Clemens Beeck
Günter Schneider (photos)

Dresden Highlights

The Practical Guide for Discovering the City

Jaron Verlag

Illustrations
Front cover: Frauenkirche
Front cover inside: Equestrian statue of Augustus the Strong
p. 2/3: Catholic Church of the Royal Court and Royal Palace
p. 6: Domes of the Frauenkirche and Art Academy with Fama statue
p. 126/127: Sculpture Collection in the Albertinum
Back cover (from top left to bottom right): Golden Rider, Zwinger, Theaterplatz,
New Synagogue

1st printing 2011
© 2011 Jaron Verlag GmbH, Berlin
(Original title: "Highlights in Dresden. Der praktische Begleiter für Entdeckungstouren durch die Stadt")
www.jaron-verlag.de
Translation: Miriamne Fields, Berlin
Map: Matthias Frach, Berlin
Cover design: rolandmdesign, Berlin, using photographs by Günter Schneider
Layout and typesetting: Prill Partners | producing, Berlin
Lithography: LVD GmbH, Berlin
Printing and Binding: Offizin Andersen Nexö Leipzig GmbH, Zwenkau

ISBN 978-3-89773-916-1
ISBN 978-3-89773-917-8 (5 copies)

Dresden's Highlights
from the Albertinum to the Zwinger

One of the loveliest cities in Europe is experiencing a Renaissance – after undergoing two decades of astonishing transformation, the city on the Elbe is becoming increasingly attractive. The reconstructed Frauenkirche has become a symbol of the return of baroque grandeur. Not only did the church give Dresden back its unmistakable silhouette, it also restored a piece of its identity. Sixty years after the city was destroyed during the bombings on February 13 and 14, 1945, Dresden's city center has reemerged in its former glory, attracting millions of people from all over the world.

At the same time that this remarkable baroque church was being rebuilt, the townhouses so characteristic of the city were also reconstructed true to the originals. These splendid baroque and rococo palaces shine once more in the historical center. The once much-acclaimed city captivates its visitors again as its buildings undergo reconstruction, one after the other.

Between the Zwinger and the Albertinum, Dresden possesses a unique flair that remains exhilarating. The sheer number of glorious buildings is fascinating. The Zwinger is the only rococo masterpiece of its kind in the world. The Cosel and Taschenberg Palaces exude dazzling noblesse. Another highpoint of the Augustus era is the richly adorned Hofkirche, the church of the royal court.

The time-honored Royal Palace with its artistic *sgraffiti* paintings recalls Dresden's architectural renown during the Renaissance. The medieval time of knights and nobility continues to live on in the Stallhof. The Brühlsche Terrasse, the balcony of Europe, is the perfect place for a stroll – between the picturesque Elbe and its breathtaking city views. The Altmarkt and Prager Strasse are both areas pulsating in the tempo of an urban shopping district.

The Neustadt allures with the formal, tranquil atmosphere of a baroque residential neighborhood. But it also contains a youthful, upbeat, trendy quarter that is both colorful and unconventional, and currently the most popular place for nightlife.

Dresden acquired the nick-name "the Florence on the Elbe" thanks both to its beauty and harmony, and to its inexhaustible wealth of cultural treasures. The Painting Gallery and Albertinum are among the leading art temples in all of Europe. The Grüne Gewölbe inside the Royal Palace is one of the most valuable collections of courtly artistic jewelry; and the porcelain collection of the legendary Elector Augustus the Strong is not to be overlooked. What is more, Dresden was a stronghold of the Romantic era, home to the painter Caspar David Friedrich and the composer Carl Maria von Weber. The city's reputation as a center of music was established by the world-famous Semper opera house. Dresden was and continues to be a city of inventors and pioneers in the fields of technology and science, demonstrated by the revolutionary Hygiene Museum and the innovative Transparent Factory. Museums like the Technological Collection testify to Dresden's leading role in the high-tech era.

If the reconstruction of the Frauenkirche is a symbol of the Dresdeners' perseverance and self-confidence, than the idyllic suburbs are an expression of their zest for life. To name just a few examples: the Loschwitz quarter, which feels both small-town and sophisticated at the same time; the enchanting Pillnitz Palace with its exotic charm; the vineyards of Radebeul – once home to Karl May – and, of course, the Moritzburg hunting palace, a jewel among the baroque palaces.

In search of the thousand-year history of the Free State of Saxony, one turns to Meissen. In this "cradle of Saxony" the authenticity of the Middle Ages can be felt everywhere. The Albrechtsburg and the cathedral are magnificent Gothic structures. Meissen porcelain has been a "hit" ever since it was invented over three hundred years ago.

To make your visit to Dresden a varied and joyful experience, this new kind of city guide provides quick and informative explanations for finding the Elbe city highlights. A brief text provides interesting information on the individual tourist attractions. A large number of brilliant photographs convey an excellent impression of what makes Dresden so magical. Addresses, opening hours and directions, a map and two registers make it easier for you to plan the details of your journey of discovery to the Florence on the Elbe.

Elegance and timelessness are part of what makes up Dresden's special aura. We made this book to ensure that you do not miss any of the city's well-known and interesting attractions. May it help you to discover one of Europe's most attractive cities!

Albertinum
Albertinum

The time-honored Albertinum, housing both the **Gallery of New Masters** and the **Sculpture Collection** has played a key role in establishing Dresden as one of the most important art centers in Europe. Since it was renovated and re-opened in 2010, the Albertinum is more impressive than ever.

This magnificently designed building already attracted attention back when it served as an armory. But today only the ground floor with its Tuscan columns and two portals remain of the original building that was erected in 1559–63 according to plans by Caspar Voigt von Wierandt.

Under the reign of King Albert of Saxony, Karl Adolf Canzler converted the building by 1887 into a museum designed in the Italian High Renaissance style.

The sculpture collection contains highly regarded works from antiquity to the present. Famous works from the Romantic period to the present are on view in the painting gallery of the new masters, including paintings by the Dresden Romantic artists, Caspar David Friedrich and Ludwig Richter. Through its collection of expressionist, constructivist and contemporary paintings, the Albertinum has become one of the most important museums of modern art.

The Albertinum is a world-famous temple of art

The new covered atrium provides space for exhibitions

Contemporary art is represented by works by Georg Baselitz

Brühlsche Terrasse/Georg-Treu-Platz
daily 10am–6pm
Tel. 49 14 20 00
www.skd.museum

▷ Tram 3, 7 (Synagoge), 1, 2, 3, 4, 7, 12 (Pirnaischer Platz)

Treasures of the sculpture collection

Albertplatz

When Erich Kästner, the famous author from Dresden, was a young boy, he enjoyed watching the busy commotion on Albertplatz, where the streets of Neutstadt converge like a star. As in former days, the round plaza continues to invite lingerers and onlookers. Two lovely **fountains**, "**Quiet Waters**" and "**Stormy Waters**" (to the west), adorn this charming landscaped plaza. The lively bronze figures were created by Robert Diez in 1893/94. Another attractive fountain on the plaza faces Königsbrücker Strasse and resembles an antique temple: The **Artesian Spring** of 1906 was made by Hans Erlwein. It recalls the original spring on Albertplatz that has been gushing forth water all the way from the Erz Mountains since 1836. It can be found in the fountain shaft beneath a small pyramid next to Dresden's first high-rise. The **Paulick High-Rise**, named after its architect, was built on Antonstrasse in 1929.

In the **Erich Kästner Museum,** a playfully presented exhibition tells visitors about the life of the famous author (1899–1974), who became known mostly for his children's books. The villa which houses the museum once belonged to Kästner's uncle.

The Erich Kästner Museum with its cozy garden

Erich Kästner Museum
Antonstrasse 1
Sun, Mon, Tues 10am–6pm; Wed 10am–8pm,
July–August: Thurs 6pm–10pm
Tel. 804 50 86
www.erich-kaestner-museum.de

▷ Tram 3, 6, 7, 8, 11 (Albertplatz)

Moving scenes depicted on the fountain created by Robert Diez

Former villa of the businessman
Eschebach (1903)

Schiller monument by Selmar
Werner (1913), on Hauptstrasse

The Altmarkt is the historic heart of Dresden. The city's oldest plaza was first mentioned in 1370 when it developed into a mercantile center with a lively market. This tradition has been continued by the **Altmarkt-Galerie**, a modern shopping center concealed behind the west side of the plaza. The Altmarkt is also where the pre-Christmas → **Striezelmarkt** takes place. The pastry shop "Konditorei Kreutzkamm," specializing in pyramid cakes, was established in 1825 when the rectangular plaza was a prestigious address.

After World War II the Altmarkt was rebuilt in the monumental style preferred by the leaders of East Germany. Baroque ornamentation was, however, added to the residential houses (1953–56). In contrast, a few of the cafés behind the arcade are presented in the look of the "swinging fifties."

The most famous structure is the **Kreuzkirche**. The church's name goes back to a religious relic – a splinter from the cross of Jesus that was donated to the church in 1234 and stored there. Founded around 1200, the church was destroyed when it came under fire by Prussian troops during the Seven Years' War. Johann Georg Schmid, Christian Friedrich Exner and Gottlob August Hölzer rebuilt it in 1764–1792 into its current form. The baroque exterior with hints of classicism, however, is contrasted

Dresdner Philharmonie Kulturpalast
Visitor Services: Mon–Fri 10am–7pm,
Sat 10am–6 pm
www.dresdnerphilharmonie.de

Kreuzkirche
daily (except Sunday) May–Oct: 10am–5pm,
Nov–March: 10am–3:30pm, April: 10am–4:30pm

▷ Tram 1, 2, 4 (Altmarkt)

The baroque Kreuzkirche seen from the Altmarkt

*The Kreuzkirche interior with its
simple postwar design*

*Monument to the church conductor,
Ernst Julius Otto (1828–75)*

*In memory of East Germany's
peace movement*

SCHWERTER
ZU PFLUGSCHAREN
FRIEDENS UND PROTEST
BEWEGUNG DIE
DAS LAND VERÄNDERTE
TAUSENDE MENSCHEN
MIT KERZEN
STIMMEN AN
DONA NOBIS PACEM

by an interior bearing the rudimentary Jugend-stil of 1900. The chimes are among the largest in Germany and for the last seven hundred years young boys have been singing in the Kreuzchor, the church's famous choir.

The **Kulturpalast**, a "palace of culture" on the border between the Altmarkt and → **Neu-markt**, is the concert hall of the Dresden Phil-harmonic symphony orchestra. The flat cube structure was built in 1962–69 according to plans by the architects Hänsch, Löschau and Zimmermann. The mural "Weg der roten Fahne," depicting socialist heroism, has been preserved on the wall facing Schlossstrasse.

The Altmarkt House was built
in 1953–56 in a baroque design

*Plenty of bargains
in the Altmarkt-Galerie*

*The Kulturpalast is the concert
hall of the Dresden philharmonic*

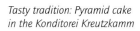

*Tasty tradition: Pyramid cake
in the Konditorei Kreutzkamm*

15

Augustusbrücke
Augustus Bridge

Everyone who walks along the Neustädter Ufer, the Elbe river embankment, is immediately charmed by the harmonious view created by the grand buildings, fields and water. Left in its natural state, the embankment plays an important role in conveying both the cityscape and spirit of Dresden – although this relationship has not always been harmonious. The city does not encroach on the river, but the Elbe has on a number of occasions crept over the riverbank, most recently in 2002 during the catastrophic "flood of the century."

During the summer the river plane across from the Altstadt turns into a large outdoor cinema.

The Augustus Bridge between Schlossplatz and Neustädter Markt is the most important of four bridges crossing the Elbe. Built in the 13th century, it was one of the first stone bridges built in central Europe and a sensation at the time. In 1727–31, Augustus the Strong had it rebuilt by Matthäus Daniel Pöppelmann and Johann Gottfried Fehre to resemble the Charles Bridge in Prague. It was redesigned in its present appearance in 1910 to allow ships to pass the first Elbe crossing. Wilhelm Kreis and Hermann Klette based the new construction on the aesthetic of Pöppelmann.

View of the Augustus Bridge with the Art Academy and Frauenkirche

The veterans of Dresden: Augustus Bridge and the paddle steamers

Schlossplatz/Neustädter Markt

www.filmnaechte-am-elbufer.de

▷ Tram 4, 8, 9 (Theaterplatz, Neustädter Markt)

*Elbe panorama between the Semper
Opera and Erlweinspeicher (right)*

Barockgarten Großsedlitz
Grosssedlitz Baroque Gardens

We can thank Augustus the Strong's irrepressible desire to build for this artistic garden before the gates of Dresden. In 1723, the Elector commissioned his best architects to create an open-air theater for his court celebrations. The Grosssedlitz Baroque Gardens, set above the Elbe valley between Heidenau and Pirna, became the most perfect French style garden in all of Saxony. Although the plans were not realized in their entirety, it remains a lovely unadulterated composition of baroque landscape design and sculptural art.

The **Upper Orangery** was created by Johann Christoph Knöffel. The curved staircase, "**Silent Music**," adorned with putti playing musical instruments, is attributed to Matthäus Daniel Pöppelmann. Zacharias Longuelune designed the elegant, well-proportioned landscaped grounds with pleasant distances and decorative fountains. A hundred and fifty bitter orange trees and three hundred potted plants are added to the arrangement in the summer.

The mostly original sandstone sculptures were created by the masters of the time, Johann Christian Kirchner and Johann Benjamin Thomae. Concerts and exhibitions take place in the Orangery and a café is open in the summertime in the **Friedrichschlösschen** (1874), a small neo-baroque palace.

Imaginative statues inhabit this landscaped garden

Parkstrasse 85
01809 Heidenau
April–August: daily 8am–8pm,
Sept–March: 8am until dusk
Tel. 0352 956 39 19
www.barockgarten-grosssedlitz.de

▷ S 1, 2 (Heidenau-Großsedlitz)

Friedrichschlösschen next to the Upper Orangery (1722)

Sphinx by the sculpture Johann Christian Kirchner

This elegant staircase leads to expansive park grounds

Blaues Wunder
Blue Wonder

The attractive area of → **Loschwitz** presents a technical sensation from the time when many groundbreaking innovations were being made. After its completion in 1893, the residents of Dresden named the elaborate bridge connecting Blasewitz and Loschwitz "Blaues Wunder," or blue wonder. It was the first time that a bridge extended across the Elbe without any river piers to support it. The engineers, Claus Köpcke and Hans Manfred Krüger, constructed this 260-meter-long turquoise structure out of 3200 tons of steel trusses. Courageous citizens were able to prevent the delicate-looking bridge from being blown up by their own troops in May 1945.

A steel wire that is almost four centimeters thick on Körnerplatz has been pulling nostalgic carriages up the mountain since 1895. The **funicular** travels 547 meters through two tunnels and covers an elevation gap of 96 meters. Just a few feet away, the world's first **suspension railway** opened in 1901. The 275 meters of tracks are supported by 33 pillars. The restored cars travel to Oberloschwitz, a neighborhood of villas situated 84 meters high.

The suspension railway ends at "Dresden's Balcony": The café and restaurant **Luisenhof** offers a fantastic view over Dresden's Elbe valley.

Funicular
Pillnitzer Landstrasse 5

Suspension railway
Körnerplatz
Tel. 0351 857 24 10
www.dvb.de

Luisenhof
Bergbahnstrasse 8
www.luisenhof.org

▷ Bus 61/83 (Körnerplatz) or Tram 6, 12
(Schillerplatz, 10 min. walk)

The Loschwitz Bridge across the
Elbe is an attraction

The suspension railway has been
operating for over a hundred years

The "Blue Wonder" bridge connects
Blasewitz (above) and Loschwitz

The sophisticated steel truss bridge
was considered a wonder in 1893

Brühlsche Terrasse

The Brühlsche Terrasse is one of the loveliest reasons to visit Dresden. High above the Elbe, alongside majestic buildings, it offers visitors a wonderful place to stroll. Heinrich Graf von Brühl (1700–1763) was responsible for transforming the massive fortress wall between Schlossplatz and → **Albertinum** into the "Balcony of Europe" in the mid-18th century. Elector Friedrich August II's prime minister was a powerful and wealthy aesthete who had his own personal realm of baroque palaces and pleasure gardens built along the river. Today the five-hundred-meter-long promenade no longer looks as it did in Brühl's time. Only the curved **Sekundogenitur**, with its mix of baroque and rococo styles, corresponds to the original buildings that once stood here. The restaurant was built in 1896/97 by the court architect Gustav Frölich.

A broad **outdoor staircase** built in 1814 leads from Schlossplatz to the terrace. Johannes Schilling (1863–68) created the sculptural group **"Four Seasons."** The first building that visitors encounter is the **Ständehaus**, Saxony's historic parliament building, erected in 1901–06 by Paul Wallot, the same architect who designed the Reichstag in Berlin. In front of the portal to today's Court of Appeals stands a monument honoring Saxony's first king, Frederick Augustus III (1750–1827). The base is a work by Karl Friedrich Schinkel and Gottfried Semper. The bronze rulers were modeled in 1843 by the sculptor Ernst Rietschel.

The Lipsius Building on the Brühlsche Terrasse resembles an antique temple

The Kunsthalle in the Lipsius Building

Kunsthalle in the Lipsius Building
Tues–Sun 10am–6pm
www.skd.museum

▷ Tram 4, 8, 9 (Theaterplatz), 3, 7 (Synagoge)

A perfect view of the Brühlsche
Terrasse along the Elbe

The **Art Academy**, known as the **Lipsius Building**, stands at the other end of the terrace. The dome of this Neo-Renaissance building created by Konstantin Lipsius (1894) with the **golden Fama**, the goddess of fame, floating above it, has become a landmark of Dresden. Changing exhibitions are presented inside the **Kunsthalle**.

Dresden's Altstadt creates a gorgeous backdrop to the Brühlsche Terrasse

The terrace ends at the garden of Count Brühl

The Saxon parliament used
to convene in the Ständehaus
on Schlossplatz

A charming setting for a café:
The neo-baroque Sekundogenitur

Centrum-Galerie
Centrum-Galerie

The **Centrum-Galerie** department store cele-
brates superlative big-city shopping. Behind
the façade's 1970's retro-look of silver-alu-
minum, a fascinating atrium opens up into
the center of the building and is framed on
all sides by an artistic, squiggly and colorful
illuminated decorative wall. The grand hall
leads to surprisingly spacious shopping levels
with modern sales areas.

This consumerism temple on Prager Strasse
is home to up to 120 different retail stores.
The architect, Peter Kulka, designed Dresden's
star shopping mall to replace the aging
Centrum-Warenhaus that once stood here.
The fashionable sparkly façade of aluminum
crystal was preserved when it was adapted
to the times and opened up. The extravagant
light metal façade from 1978 was the idea
of the Hungarian architects Ferenc Simon and
Ivan Fokvari.

*The merchandise is
presented in a brilliantly
designed interior*

Prager Strasse 12
Mon–Sat 9:30am–8pm
www.centrumgalerie.de

▷ Tram 8, 9, 11, 12 (Prager Strasse)

*Rococo-like decor adorns
the department store*

*A shopping palace clad
in glitter on Prager Strasse*

Coselpalais
Cosel Palace

Behind the Frauenkirche stands a magnificent example of baroque Dresden. The bright yellow city palace and courtyard were built for Frederick August von Cosel, the son of Anna Constanze, the Countess of Cosel, who was August the Strong's famous mistress.

The stately aristocratic palace is a highly admired jewel of late baroque architecture. Richly decorated, it displays the coat of arms of its landlord, a general, in the triangular gable.

The two flat side wings and the fence adorned with fanciful putty are all that survived the Second World War. The five-story Cosel Palace was rebuilt from 1998 to 2000 according to the original designs by Christian Gottfried Hahmann. The staircase and ballroom situated behind the round and oval windows are presented in the original historical style. During reconstruction, parts of the medieval city walls were discovered and integrated into the cellar. A restaurant called "**Pulverturm**" is located in the vaults of the former powder tower.

Evidence of past glory and grandness: the Cosel Palace in the Altstadt

Café in the tasteful ambience of the palace

An der Frauenkirche 12

▷ Tram 1, 2, 3, 4, 7, 12 (Pirnaischer Platz)

Baroque wall fountain in the courtyard of Gottfried Knöffler's palace

Elbschlösser
Elbe Palaces

The hillside above the Elbe offers a stunning view of the Elbe palaces, in particular the impressive **Albrechtsberg Palace**. It was built for the Prussian prince Heinrich Albrecht who, after marrying a woman out of keeping with his position, was forced to turn his back on his homeland. The prince commissioned Adolf Lohse, a pupil of the famous building master Schinkel, to create this complex in the Italian Renaissance style. Since 1854 the Hohenzollern "asylum" has towered majestically over the river where → **paddle steamers** still travel today. The couple had a hundred rooms at their disposal including the regal Crown Hall. The terraces and stairs on the sloping hillside are also arranged artistically.

The prince had a villa erected next door for his chamberlain Baron von Stockhausen. The **Villa Stockhausen**, created in 1853 in the style of late classicism, was also a work of Lohse. The industrialist Karl August Lingner (known for Odol mouthwash) bought it in 1906. The famous pharmaceutical entrepreneur who died in 1916 is buried in a small mausoleum at the bank of the Elbe.

The palace trio is completed up river by the **Eckberg Palace**, built in 1861 by Christian Friedrich Arnold for the businessman Johann Souchay. This Neo-Gothic structure in the Tudor style now operates as a luxury hotel.

Romantic palace panorama above the Elbe, near Neustadt

The Eckberg Palace is a Neo-Gothic work of art

Bautzener Strasse 130, 132, 134

Albrechtsberg Palace
Group tours
www.schloss-albrechtsberg.de

▷ Tram 11 (Elbschlösser)

Glorious palace for Prussia's
princes: Albrechtsberg Castle

Villa Stockhausen, also known
as the Lingner Palace

31

Festung Dresden
Fortress of Dresden

When wandering through the **Brühlscher Garden**, few are aware of the stone labyrinth under their feet. The ruins of the former fortress of Dresden lie hidden beneath the park's plateau. There is much to discover in the "underground" museum, including the "Ziegeltor" – the oldest preserved city gate – with its connecting stone bridge across the fortress moat, the canon courts and the casemates of the Venus Bastion.

The Renaissance fortress was built in 1546 under the reign of the future Elector Moritz. Following plans drawn up by Caspar Voigt von Wierandt, a massive wall was built around the city following an Italian model. The Venus Bastion at the Elbe river bank was added in 1590 and given to Premier Minister Count Heinrich von Brühl in 1748 as a gift. He had it converted into landscaped gardens. The entrance to the fortress is located at the staircase next to the **Kunsthalle**.

On the Elbe side of the bastion corner facing the Carola Bridge stands the oldest monument in Dresden (a copy). The **Moritz Monument** of 1555 commemorates Moritz of Saxony, the man who had the fortress built. It depicts Moritz, who came from the House of Wettin, handing over the Saxon sword to his successor and brother. The dynamic sculpture was made by Hans Walther II.

Georg-Treu-Platz
April–Oct: daily 10am–6pm
Nov–March: daily 10am–5pm
Tel. 438 37 03 12
www.schloesser-dresden.de

▷ Tram 3, 7 (Synagoge)

The Moritz monument is
Dresden's oldest memorial

The entrance to the fortress
beneath the Brühlsche Garden

Great canon court and passageways in the Renaissance fortress

Frauenkirche
Frauenkirche

The Frauenkirche is *the* symbol of Dresden: The church embodies the glorious era of Augustus; as a ruin it recalled the destruction of 1945; since 1993 it has served as an example of public spirit set in stone.

The reconstruction of the church that was destroyed in World War II was supported by a private initiative and completed in 2005. It also triggered the revival of the → **Neumarkt** district.

The Protestant Frauenkirche with its bell-shaped dome was first built in 1726–43 according to plans by George Bähr (1666–1738), whose grave is located inside the crypt. The house of worship with the bold sandstone dome (26 meters in diameter) is one of the most important baroque structures in Europe. A spiral ramp leads to a viewing platform 67 meters high. The church, when measured with the dome's cross that was forged in London, measures 91 meters.

The circular nave with the four galleries set over one another is also unusual. The dome mural depicts the four Evangelicals. Christoph Wetzel painted them from the original by Giovanni Battista Grone.

The altar from 1739 (Johann Christian Feige the elder and Benjamin Thomae) was reconstructed from 2000 pieces of rubble. One fourth of the new Frauenkirche consists of building material from the original.

The Frauenkirche on Neumarkt shining in its former glory

Imposing inner dome above the hall with the four evangelicals

Neumarkt/An der Frauenkirche
Mon–Fri 10am–12pm, 1pm–6pm
Frauenkirche visitors' center in the Kulturpalast
www.frauenkirche-dresden.de

▷ Tram 1, 2, 4 (Altmarkt)

The dome above the city

Church hall with altar and organ

Fürstenzug
Procession of the Princes

The Fürstenzug is probably the best-attended history lesson in the world: The 102-meter-long mural along the wall of the **Langer Gang (long arcade)** on Auguststrasse is a gallery of ancestral portraits depicting the Saxonrulers mounted on horseback and forming a guard of honor. Almost all the Wettiners are assembled here, from Conrad the Great (1123–56) to Frederick Augustus III (1904–18). Royalty is joined by respected artists and scholars at the end of the procession. After the original mural, applied with a *sgraffito* technique by the history painter Wilhelm Walther in 1872–76, had weathered, the figures were eternalized on Meissner porcelain in 1907. This was a wise decision: The 24,000 tiles survived the inferno during the bombardment of Dresden in February 1945.

No doubt many of the gentlemen shown in the mural participated in the medieval competitions that were held in the **Stallhof**, the show grounds behind the monumental picture. The 16th century **competition track** has been preserved in its entirety, including the two six-meter-high bronze columns used for ring lancing, a traditional medieval sport. The arcade, decorated with antlers and coat of arms, has connected the → **Royal Palace** with the → **Johanneum** since 1591 and was designed by the Italian Giovanni Maria Nosseni.

The Stallhof behind the Langer Gang

Augustusstrasse

▷ Tram 4, 8, 9 (Theaterplatz)

Saxon history preserved on Meissen porcelain at the Langer Gang

*Elector Augustus the Strong
(1670–1733) and his son
Frederick Augustus II*

Gartenstadt Hellerau
Garden City of Hellerau

A hundred years ago, Hellerau was a synonym for a progressive lifestyle in everyday life, work, and culture. Much of what was developed at that time seems perfectly normal today, for example, the first garden city established in Germany. Karl Schmidt, a socially-active furniture manufacturer, initiated the project in 1909 when he moved his **German workshops** to a model factory outside the city. Soon construction of the idyllic garden city began, following a general plan developed by Richard Riemerschmid that extended from Am Grünen Zipfel to the Markt.

The **Festspielhaus**, a festival hall, was an international sensation when it opened in 1912. Émile Jaques-Dalcroze, from Switzerland, established the "Educational Center for Rhythmic Gymnastics" there to teach experimental dance. The innovative cultural building was constructed by Heinrich Tessenow without a stage podium, orchestra pit or separate spectator area. Over time Hellerau became a mecca for the avant-garde.

Today the **European Center for the Arts in Dresden** carries on this tradition. With festivals outside mainstream entertainment and presentations of all too serious high culture, Hellerau and its Festspielhaus are once again a popular site for contemporary music and dance.

A legend of the cultural avant-garde: Hellerau festival hall

European Center for the Arts in Dresden
Karl-Liebknecht-Strasse 56
Tues–Fr 10am–4pm
Tel. 264 62 23
www.hellerau.org

Deutsche Werkstätten
Moritzburger Weg 67

▷ Tram 8 (Am Hellerrand, Festspielhaus Hellerau)

Idyllic beauty in Germany's first garden city

Once revolutionary: small houses for small budgets

Entrance gate to the courtyard of the German workshops

Gemäldegalerie Alte Meister
Painting Gallery of Old Masters

This is one of the most important painting collections in the world. Many of the paintings on display are classic works of art history. Visitors to the Painting Gallery of Old Masters are fascinated by Raphael's "Sistine Madonna," Giorgione's "Sleeping Venus" and Titian's "The Tribute Money." In addition to other classical works of the Renaissance and Italian baroque period, the museum exhibits master works of 17th century Flemish and Dutch painters such as Rembrandt, Rubens, Vermeer and van Dyck. The collection contains German painting up to the 18th century, including treasures by Cranach the elder and Albrecht Dürer, as well as superb works by French and Spanish artists of the 17th century. Of course the famous views of Dresden painted by Bernardo Bellotto, known as Canaletto, are also on display.
This temple of art designed in Italian High Renaissance style was built on Theaterplatz in 1847–55 by Dresden's famous architect Gottfried Semper. He delicately set the Painting Gallery onto the open space to the north of the → Zwinger. With this sandstone building Semper created one of the grandest European museums of the 19th century and established a style that would become highly influential.

Raphael's "Sistine Madonna" is a highlight of the collection

Gottfried Semper designed the important Painting Gallery

Theaterplatz 1
Tues–Sun 10am–6pm
Tel. 49 14 20 00
www.sdk.museum

▷ Tram 4, 8, 9 (Theaterplatz)

Europe's painting masters on three levels under one roof

*Paintings hung in two rows
just as Semper envisioned*

Gläserne Manufaktur
Transparent Factory

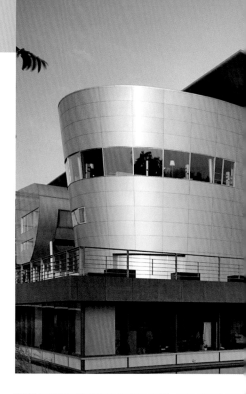

When fans of luxury cars come here, their eyes light up. Not only is a VW luxury car assembled by hand in the Transparent Factory, buyers and interested visitors are able to watch as the cars are assembled.

The production takes place in an aesthetically pleasing atmosphere. The workers show their skills on the parquet floor. The limousine is presented as a luxurious one-of-a-kind piece, a world apart from mass-produced automobiles. The finished car bodies are piled up in a forty-meter-high glass tower that resembles a modern shrine. The lavish automobiles may be tried out on a driving simulator and buyers can assemble their car according to their individual wishes on computers.

The factory, which opened at the turn of the millennium on the northern corner of the → **Grosser Garten**, is a symbol of the new Dresden. The local architect Gunter Henn erected the progressive production site completely out of glass, with a visitors' center set behind two aluminum structures.

VW provides information about its production in the Visitor Forum

Lennéstrasse 1
Tours offered daily from 10am to 5pm. Reservation required at 01805 89 62 68 or by email: infoservice@glaesernemanufaktur.de

▷ Tram 1, 2, 4, 10, 12, 13 (Strassburger Platz)

The manufacturer's futuristic look with glass shelves of automobiles

One more check before the final inspection

No trace of factory left: Car assembly on the parquet floor

Großer Garten
Great Garden

The largest park in Dresden, with its special mix of baroque glory and diverse leisure activities, offers something for everyone. The first green area was created in 1676; the network of pathways was added in 1683 according to plans by Johann Friedrich Karcher. Two hundred years later Karl Friedrich Bouché landscaped the public park in the style of an English garden.

The first baroque structure built in Saxony stands at the center of the park grounds. Johann Georg Starcke built a **palace** for Elector Johann Georg III in 1678–83 in the French style with rich façade ornamentation. Very dynamic baroque marble statues are dispersed around the seat of nobility on Hauptallee. Today the palace is also used as a venue for special events held in the park.

In the 19th century, part of the park was converted into a **zoo** and **botanical gardens**. Open-air stages such as the **Parktheater am Palaisteich** or the **Puppet Theater** are very popular. Nearby a youth ecological house and a café have been set up in the **Carola-schlösschen** by the lake.

This huge area of green can be explored comfortably during the summer months with the **park train**. Two miniature locomotives from 1925 pull the narrow gauge train to all the park's attractions.

Zoo
Tiergartenstrasse 1
daily 8:30am until dusk
www.zoo-dresden.de

Botanical Gardens
Stübelallee 2
daily 8am–6pm, Oct–March: 10am until dusk
www.tu-dresden.de

▷ Tram 10, 13 (Großer Garten), 9, 13 (Zoo)

Giraffes and zebra in the Dresden zoo

The palace in the Great Garden
brought the baroque to Dresden

Tropical water plants
in the botanical gardens

Steam locomotive in miniature: The
park railroad in the Great Garden

45

Hygiene-Museum, Deutsches
Hygiene Museum, German

The Dresden Hygiene Museum, presenting far more than just remarkable views of the human body's insides, is known well beyond the city limits. The entire focus here is on the physical existence of humans, with exhibits on "eating and drinking," "motion," "beauty, skin and hair" and "sexuality."

The museum was founded over a hundred years ago by the manufacturer Karl August Lingner, whose mouthwash "Odol" became an international success. His interest was in raising his fellow citizens' awareness of a healthy body.

The museum building's neo-classical functional architecture was designed by Wilhelm Kreis and set on the visual axis of the → **Great Garden.** When it opened in 1930, the "glass woman" was a sensation. A transparent life-size doll whose organs, bones, nerve tract and blood stream are clearly visible, the latter made of 13 kilometers of copper wire!

The permanent exhibition titled "Human Adventure" is presented in an entertaining way using modern exhibition techniques. Museum visitors get a sense of what it is like to be blind or as old as a stone. The German Hygiene Museum maintains more than 1,300 exhibition objects.

Nutrition is one of the themes addressed in the Hygiene Museum

Lingnerplatz 1
Tues–Sun 10am–6pm
Tel. 48 46 400
www.dhmd.de

▷ Tram 10, 13 (Großer Garten); 1, 2, 4, 12 (Deutsches Hygiene-Museum)

The "Glass Woman" has been the major attraction since 1930

The Hygiene Museum with the statue of the "Ball Thrower"

The miracle of life, enlarged and vivid

Jägerhof
Jägerhof

Martin Luther was an important guest of the Augustinian cloister that once stood here. After the monks gave up their refuge, Elector Augustus of Saxony built the **Jägerhof** here in 1582. The spacious grounds were cut back in the 19th century until all that remained was the stately west wing on Köpckestrasse. It is a typical Renaissance structure with a decorated gable and three striking staircase towers on the outside of the building. Built in 1617, it now houses the **Museum of Saxon Folk Art** with decorative arts originating from the Erz Mountains, the Vogtland region and the Sorbian Lausitz. The **Puppet Theater Collection**, the only one of its kind in the world, maintains a fascinating and fanciful collection of marionettes, hand, rod and stick puppets from three centuries as well as play figures from the Far East.

Two large stately buildings were erected on the large grounds of the hunting lodge on the Elbe: the **Finance Ministry** (1894) and today's **Saxon State Chancellery** (1904) on Carolaplatz.

The folklore museum shows an original farmhouse parlor

Smoking men and nutcrackers from the Erz Mountains

Museum of Saxon Folk Art with Puppet Theater Collection
Köpckestrasse 1
Tues–Sun 10am–6pm
Tel. 49 14 20 00
www.sdk.museum

▷ Tram 4, 8, 9 (Neustädter Markt); 3, 7, 8 (Carolaplatz)

*Imposing Finance Ministry
at the Neustädter Ufer*

*The Jägerhof goes back to the
glorious period of the Renaissance*

Japanisches Palais
Japanese Palace

Elector Augustus the Strong (1670–1733) had hoped to fulfill two dreams with this palace: He wanted the Japanese Palace on the Neustadt side to be part of a stately city backdrop along the Elbe River comparable to the Canale Grande in Venice. He also wanted the interior clad entirely in porcelain. In 1728–33 the Elector's architects, Matthäus Daniel Pöppelmann, Jean de Bodt and Zacharias Longuelune, succeeded in creating a masterful baroque palace. In addition to the curved rooftops, a row of herma sculptures of funny Chinese figures stand in the inner courtyard and contribute to the exotic Asian flair.

By 1786 the Japanese Palace was already serving as a museum and fifty years later Gottfried Semper redesigned a few of its rooms in the style of antiquity.

Today the **Museum of Ethnology**, **the Senckenberg Natural History Collection** and the **State Museum of Pre-History** display their treasures in changing exhibitions. Visitors can enjoy the famous "Canaletto View" from the back garden. In 1748, the Venetian artist Bernardo Bellotto, referred to as Canaletto, stood at this site when he painted what is probably the most famous view of Dresden.

Baroque palace in Japanese style in Dresden's Neustadt

Sea dwellers in the Senckenberg Collection

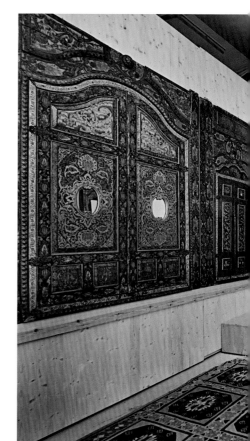

Palaisplatz 11
Tues–Sun 10am–6pm
Tel. 81 44 860
www.voelkerkunde-dresden.de

▷ Tram 4, 9 (Palaisplatz)

Chinese people adorning the
façade in the palace courtyard

The glorious "Damascus Room"
in the Museum of Ethnology

Johanneum
Johanneum

At one time the Electors parked their horses and coaches here; now it is home to the Methuselah of modern mobility. The **Transport Museum** in the Johanneum shows veterans of the early modern age of locomotion, including the "Muldenthal," the oldest preserved original from a steam locomotive in Germany, dating back to 1861.

Numerous vintage cars, especially from the past automobile industry in East Germany and Saxony, are on view. Hans Grade's "monoplane" goes back to the early days of flying. The collection of old bicycles is another impressive exhibit.

The Johanneum was built as stables in 1586–91 by Paul Buchner. The original Renaissance portal has been preserved. Its resemblance to a palace goes back to its interim use as a painting gallery in the mid-18th century. Johann Christoph Knöffel converted the building into its current appearance in 1744–46. The oldest object in the museum, a sedan chair from 1705, also dates back to this period. The last cosmetic alterations were carried out in 1872–76 by Karl Moritz Haenel in the Neo-Renaissance style.

Passenger transport in the Johanneum during the time of the German Reich

On the ground and in the air:
Old-timers as far as the eye can see

Augustusstrasse 1
Tues–Sun 10am–5pm
Tel. 86 44 0
www.verkehrsmuseum-dresden.de

▷ Tram 1, 2, 4 (Altmarkt)

Dresden's steam paddlers –
and their Mississippi relatives

The Johanneum – an elegant
building of the Saxon court

Curious carriages in
a contemporary workshop

Karl-May-Museum
Karl May Museum

Millions of readers from all over the world were captivated by his adventure novels. Almost every child in Germany is familiar with Old Shatterhand, Winnetou and Kara Ben Nemsi, the heroes of his books who continue to live on today.

Since 1890 Karl May (1842–1912) has been one of the most-read German authors. Following his success late in life, he moved from Dresden to Radebeul in 1896, where he built his **Villa Shatterhand**.

Now the legendary props from his fantasy world, such as Old Shatterhand's suit, the "Silver Nails Rifle" and the "Henry Short Rifle," can be seen in the popular author's private home: The exhibition presents the life and work of the author displaying objects in the library and study, which is furnished in an oriental style.

The **Villa Bärenfett** right next door focuses on the protagonists of western epics, the North American Indians. With more than eight hundred artifacts, it is one of the most valuable collections of an indigenous people and vividly conveys the everyday life and culture of the native Americans. The German artist Patty Frank collected clothing, headdresses, tomahawks and peace pipes during his guest performances in North America. The museum in the log cabin was founded in 1928.

Villa Shatterhand in Radebeul, the best-selling author's hideaway

Karl-May-Strasse 5
01445 Radebeul
Tues–Sun, Mar–Oct: 9am–6pm, Nov–Feb: 10am–4pm
Tel. 837 30 10
www.karl-may-museum.de

▷ S 1 (Radebeul-Ost), Tram 4 (Schildenstrasse)

Valuable attire of the North America's natives

World-famous weapons from the imagined world of Karl May

Karl May's study and desk

Katholische Hofkirche
Catholic Church of the Royal Court

Effectively displayed on a highly exposed site, it dominates the silhouette of the city on the Elbe. The St. Trinitatis Catholic church on Schlossplatz impressively demonstrates the strong influence of Italian artists in Dresden. The architect Gaetano Chiaveri from Rome began building this masterpiece in the late Roman baroque style in 1739. Its solemn radiance is further augmented by the 78 sculptures (59 of them representing saints) created by Lorenzo Mattielli.

The delicate, free-standing tower above the bold portal façade became an influential style in Dresden.

The church of the royal court, completed in 1755 in a heartland of the Reformation, has a notable history: Elector Augustus the Strong converted to Catholicism in 1697 so that he could become king of Poland. This is why he was buried in Cracau. Only his heart was preserved in the Dresden cathedral. The crypt of the church holds 49 sarcophagi of the Wettin dynasty.

Out of respect to the Protestant citizens, the processional path was placed within the church with a bridge connecting the church to the palace.

The attractive pulpit was made by the master sculptor Balthasar Permoser, and the highly gifted organ builder, Johann Gottfried Silbermann, left his last and largest organ to the cathedral (1750–53).

Pulpit designed by Balthasar Permoser (1710) and the Silbermann organ

Schlossplatz/Theaterplatz
www.bistum-dresden-meissen.de

▷ Tram 4, 8, 9 (Theaterplatz)

56

The baroque cathedral next to the palace's Hausmann Tower

The altar picture was painted by Anton Raphael Mengs in 1752 in Rome

Kurländer Palais
Kurländer Palace

Compared to the majestic villas around the Frauenkirche, the Kurländer Palace on the edge of the Altstadt appears rather modest. Built in 1729 for the Count of Wackerbarth, the delicate but very dignified facade is an example of Dresden's restrained rococo. The architect Johann Christoph Knöffel was a master of refined understatement and his work was considered the "loveliest palace" in Dresden.

The Point de vue at the end of Rampische Strasse has an interesting history. It was owned and named after Prince Karl of Saxony, the Duke of Kurland, in 1774.

Doctors began to move here in the early 19th century and in 1815 Christian Friedrich Schuricht founded the first Surgical Medical Academy. Carl Gustav Carus (1789–1869), the king's personal physician and a Romantic painter, had his medical practice inside the palace.

The war ruin was rebuilt into a palace again in 2008, and one of the city's best restaurants opened there. Guests can dine inside, amidst bare plaster walls, or outside, in an Italian-style arcade court.

The vestibule in the Kurländer Palace with a modern interior

Tzschirnerplatz 3–5
Restaurant Kastenmeier
daily 12pm–11pm
www.kastenmeiers.de

▷ Tram 3, 7 (Synagoge)

Fine dining in the newly designed rooms

Elegant original façade from the rococo era

59

Landesbibliothek
State Library

Everything revolves around the book – regardless of whether it is in a library of impressive architecture or a museum containing precious scripts. The national, state and university library that opened in 2003 is not only a mecca for book worms, it also attracts fans of modern architecture. The architects Ortner and Ortner lowered the reading room into the ground. After all, set four levels below surface, beneath a glass roof and surrounded by warm wood tones, it guarantees an atmosphere conducive to learning. Above ground the library can be recognized by the two travertine-clad blocks whose façades resemble bookshelves. The **Book Museum**, housed in the upper section of the library building, contains wonderful treasures from the earliest period of recorded words and pictures. Its most famous artifacts include the Dresden Maya Manuscript from the 13th century, the Mainz Psaltery of 1457 and the "Sachsenspiegel" – the oldest German law code. There is also a sketch book from Albrecht Dürer, Bach's mass in B minor and the German version of Maria Sybilla Merian's "New Book of Flowers." The idea for the museum goes back to the Dresden author Erich Kästner.

Only part of the State Library is above ground

Devout atmosphere in Dresden's new book temple

Zellerscher Weg 18
Mon–Sat 10am–5pm
Tel: 467 75 80
www.slub-dresden.de

▷ Tram 3, 8 (Nürnberger Platz), Bus 61
(Staats- und Universitätsbibliothek)

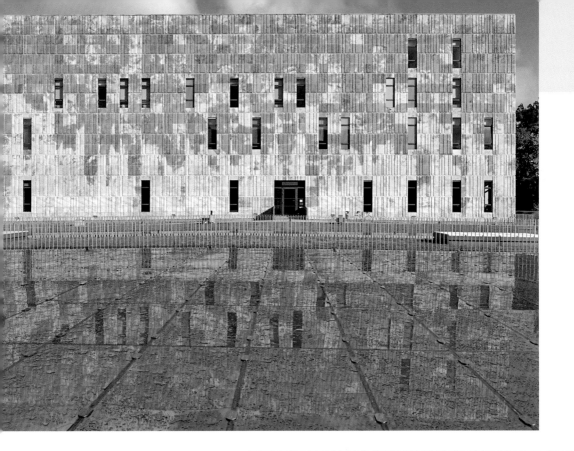

*Valuable manuscripts in the book
museum's treasure chamber*

*The library reading room
is located underground*

Landhaus
Landhaus

This historically important and architecturally unique country house is the residence of the **Stadtmuseum Dresden**, Dresden's city museum. The Saxon state parliament, made up of representatives of the different estates, once convened here and the state tax administration also had its offices here. In 1770–75, the Dresden court architect Friedrich August Krubsacius (1718–1789) created both an imposing and elegant building, influenced by the French style. On the Landhausstrasse he created the first classicist façade in Dresden. The staircase hall, however, is designed in the style of a lively baroque palace.

The City Museum presents more than eight hundred years of history of the city on the Elbe. It exhibits precious documentation of Dresden's rise and haunting memories of the city's destruction. It also addresses life under dictatorships in the 20th century.

The Städtische Galerie Dresden, a high quality art collection, is located in the same building. It shows "Masterpieces of Dresden" from the 20th century to the present as well as works by local artists such as Otto Dix, Thoralf Knobloch and A. R. Penck.

A model of historic Dresden displayed in the City Museum in the Landhaus

Stadtmuseum & Städtische Galerie
Wilsdruffer Strasse 2
Tues–Sun 10am–6pm, Fridays until 7pm
Tel. 488 73 70
www.museen-dresden.de

▷ Tram 1, 2, 3, 4, 7, 12 (Pirnaischer Platz)

The main staircase is worth
a look

Contemporary art in
the Städtischen Galerie

Saxon's parliament convened
here until 1907; today it is the
City Museum

Loschwitz
Loschwitz

The splendid atmosphere of this idyllic site was even enjoyed by Friedrich Schiller. In 1785–87, the poet found inspiration for his drama "Don Carlos" in the garden house of his friend Christian Gottfried Körner's vineyard. He is commemorated today by the little **Schiller House**. Not far way, George Bähr, the architect of the famous Frauenkirche, created his first house of worship, the baroque **Loschwitz Church**, in 1708. A number of artists were attracted to Loschwitz after the vineyard had to be given up in 1870. Eduard Leonhardi, the Late Romantic painter, for example, erected a picturesque studio house in the valley along Grundstrasse. The **Leonhardi Museum**, whose exterior is covered in worldly wisdoms, shows works by the Late Romantic artist as well as contemporary art. Wealthy citizens built themselves posh villas above Loschwitz on the hillside named "White Deer." The number of architectural styles represented in the upscale "Gold Dust Quarter" is overwhelming. The most interesting mansions are Villa San Remo (Bergbahnstrasse 12), Villa Eschebach (Lahmannring 3) and Villa Artushof (Malerstrasse 18). The former spa hotel of 1874 stands on Bautzner Landstrasse (6a) – adorned with a sculpture of a white dear. At one time Loschwitz was a very popular spa.

Schillerhäuschen
Schillerstrasse 19
May–Sept. Sat/Sun 10am–5pm
Tel. 488 73 70
www.museen-dresden.de

Leonhardi-Museum
Grundstrasse 26
Tues–Fri 2pm–6pm, Sat/Sun 10am–6pm
Tel. 268 35 13
www.leonhardi-museum.de

▷ Bus 61/83 (Körnerplatz) or Tram 6, 12 (Schillerplatz, 10 minute walk)

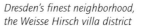

Romantic storybook house: the Leonhardi Museum

Dresden's finest neighborhood, the Weisse Hirsch villa district

Small garden house for a great mind: the little Schiller House

*The Loschwitz Church nestled
in the slope of the Elbe*

Meißen
Meissen

The city of Meissen, located about 25 kilometers downriver from the center of the Saxon capital, is closely linked to the history of Dresden. The dynasty of the House of Wettin began here in 1089. The "cradle of Saxony" preserved its medieval cityscape. The Albrechtsburg Castle and the cathedral are picturesquely elevated on Burgberg, the hill above the Altstadt and the Elbe.

Albrechtsburg Castle, begun in 1471, is believed to be the first palace structure erected in Germany. The **Große Wendelstein,** a sandstone staircase tower on the church plaza, was a masterful architectural accomplishment at the time. Arnold von Westfalen created the Gothic palace and Jakob Heilmann continued work on it in 1521. The magnificent painting and decoration of the large rooms is the work of Wilhelm Rossmann and Ernst Haendel and dates back to 1873–85.

The Meissen **cathedral** stands behind the palace and is the most important medieval structure in Saxony. Construction of the Gothic cathedral began around 1250 and was completed around 1390. The superb sculptures of the Naumburg Master (around 1260) are found there as well. The delicate twin towers

Striking silhouette across the Elbe: the Burgberg of Meissen

The Brauhaus in the Altstadt with a Renaissance gable

Imposing Meissen town hall of 1472–80 on the market square

Albrechtsburg
Domplatz 1
daily 10am–6pm

Cathedral
Domplatz 7
daily Apr–Oct: 9am–6pm, Nov–March: 10am–4pm

Meissen City Museum
Heinrichsplatz 3
daily 11am–5pm
Tel. 03521 45 88 57
www.touristinfo-meissen.de

Filigree cathedral tower with the chapel in front

were built in 1904–08 in the Neo-Gothic style.
The original towers had collapsed by 1413.
The **Bischofsburg**, several **manor houses** and
the **Kornhaus** enclose the Burgberg ensemble.
The imposing **Rathaus**, the town hall built in
1472–80, stands on the Market Square in the
lower part of town. Arnold von Westfalen also
contributed to its realization. The high attic
of the building was once used to store grain.
Elegant townhouses and artisan buildings
dominate the quarter around the square and
the Burgstrasse. The Renaissance gable of the
Brauhaus (1569), next to the **Frauenkirche**,
is particularly lovely. The porcelain chimes
hang in the tower of this 16th century house of
worship. Steps lead from here to the **St. Afra
Church** (Freiheit 15) that was built around
1300.

*Hall inside the Albrechtsburg
Castle with historic paintings
from 1873–85*

*Picturesque manor houses on
the Burgberg with restaurants*

Gothic architecture in the Great
Room of the Albrechtsburg Castle

The gatehouse leads to the
Burgberg above the old town

Meissner Porzellan-Manufaktur
Meissen Porcelain Factory

World famous and valuable – Europe's oldest porcelain continues to fascinate. The original ceramic ware with the blue swords emblem has been a status symbol and a luxury item for three hundred years. In the Meissen Porcelain Factory visitors can see how the "white gold" is transformed into unique artwork. Workshops demonstrate the most important stations of production, forming and spinning, figure modeling, and glazing, which requires adroit hands and a delicate touch. About three thousand pieces of porcelain are on display in the Meissen House, demonstrating a wealth of ideas and diversity of styles from the earliest days of production to the present. Not only porcelain lovers are amazed by the porcelain zoo, the mountings for precious stones, and the brilliant 3.5-meter-high centerpiece from 1749 that once belonged to Elector Frederick Augustus II.

The European porcelain has many inventors: In addition to Gottfried Pabst von Ohain and Walter von Tschirnhaus, Johann Friedrich Böttger also managed to produce the precious china after many years of experimentation. A short time later, in 1710, Augustus the Strong founded the Porcelain Factory, which was located in the medieval Albrechtsburg castle until 1864.

The worldwide demand for Meissen's famous porcelain is immense

Haus Meissen
Talstrasse 9
May–Oct: daily 9am–6pm, Nov–April: daily 9am–5pm
www.meissen.com

▷ S 1 (Meißen-Triebischtal)

This table centerpiece is a highlight of the porcelain museum

Modern visitors' center in
the Meissen factory

A glimpse over the shoulder:
artistic glaze painting

Militärhistorisches Museum
Military History Museum

The museum of military history in Germany, which has existed for almost a hundred years, presents itself in a new appearance and with a new concept. The exhibit now focuses on people, for example, through vivid drawings of soldiers on the front. The new building extension designed by the American architect Daniel Libeskind also demonstrates a new perspective. A metal wedge provocatively breaks through the rigid façade of the German empire armory (1875) – the internationally acclaimed architect's way of illustrating that war is "organized violence."

The most important museum of the Bundeswehr is also the largest one in Germany. The first submarine of 1851 is on display, along with the "Lazy Maidservant," a huge cannon from 1450, and the spacesuit of Sigmund Jähn, Germany's first astronaut (1978). The barracks of the Albertstadt were built in 1873–80. When bombs fell on Dresden in February 1945, the garrison was left unscathed. The **Garnisonskirche** is also an interesting church. Dedicated in 1900, it was used both for Protestant and Catholic prayer services. The Neo-Romantic dual-use church was designed by Lossow and Viehweger.

A contrast of old and new: Museum with Daniel Libeskind's extension

The impressive Garnison Church was built for the military barracks complex

Olbrichtplatz 2
To open at the end of 2011
Tel. 823 28 03
www.mhm.bundeswehr.de

▷ Tram 7, 8 (Stauffenbergallee)

A tank for beginner drivers stands in the viewing depot

Sigmund Jähn's landing spacecraft "Soyuz"

Prussian spiked helmet from the time of the German Empire

Moritzburg
Moritzburg

A work out of a picture book that connects stately beauty with perfectly composed nature: The imposing Wasserschloss Moritzburg, a palace surrounded by water, is the highpoint of the marvelous cultural landscape north of Dresden. Augustus the Strong had the baroque hunting and summer palace built in 1723–33 by the Matthäus Daniel Pöppelmann, who remodeled the original castle (1546) that had belonged to Duke Moritz. The corner towers that were already in place were adjusted to the baroque ideal. The magnificent castle chapel with ridge turrets already existed, created by Wolf Caspar Klengel in 1672.

The landlord, depicted as a horn-blowing hunter, greets the new arrival personally at the entrance to the castle. Places of interest in the palace include the **Porcelain Quarter** and the Feather Room of Augustus the Strong: A state bed and patterned tapestry are made of more than a million bird feathers (1720). The castle halls are decorated with countless deer antlers. The **Pheasant Palace** is a 40 minute walk from here, located on a lake called Niederer Groß-teich. The romantic palace designed in pink tones was built in 1770–1776 under Elector Frederick Augustus III according to plans by Johann Daniel Schades, who also created the lake piers with the **lighthouse** (1780).

The Pheasants Palace is a treasure in Moritzburg

Moritzburg Castle
April–Oct: daily 10am–5pm; Nov–Jan 10: Tues–Sun 10am–4pm; Feb/March: Sat/Sun 10am–4pm
Porcelain Quarter
April–Oct: 11am–4pm; Nov. to Mar. Sat/Sun 11am–2pm
Pheasant Palace
April–Oct: daily 10am–5pm
Tel. 352 077 30
www.schloss-moritzburg.de

▷ Bus 326, 457, 458, narrow gauge train from Radebeul-Ost (S 1)

*Moritzburg castle and chapel
with high ridge turrets*

*A collection of deer antlers
unique to Europe*

*The fascinating "feather room" with
Augustus the Strong's regal bed*

Neue Synagoge
New Synagogue

The Jewish community of Dresden returned to its original location on the Elbe in 2001. The New Synagogue's two striking cube structures are elevated on the eastern side of the → **Brühlsche Terrasse**. The award-winning ensemble consisting of the community center and windowless synagogue was designed by the office of Wandel, Hoefer, Lorch and Hirsch from Saarbrücken.

The original building of 1840 was a work of Gottfried Semper, who also provided Dresden with its world-renowned opera house, situated just down the river. The original synagogue was set on fire by the Nazis during the pogrom night of November 9, 1938. The badly-damaged building was later torn down. A seven-branched menorah commemorates this event at the former entrance.

The New Synagogue's sandstone cube shifts, layer for layer, until it is entirely facing eastward, the traditional orientation of a Jewish place of worship. The Star of David is exhibited at the entrance. The building also encompasses biblical references: The stone enclosure represents Solomon's temple. The sanctuary is enclosed by a thin metallic curtain symbolizing the tabernacle.

The community center and café are located on the other side of the courtyard that is designed with a grove of sycamore trees.

The inscription reads "My house is a house of prayer for all peoples"

Hasenberg / Rathenauplatz
Tours: Tel. 656 07 20
www.hatikva.de,

Café Schoschana, Sun–Thurs 12pm–6pm

▷ Tram 3, 7 (Synagogue)

Fine metallic curtain encloses the prayer room of the synagogue

The massive cube of the New
Synagogue revolves around itself

The glassed-in community
center across the courtyard

Neumarkt

The extremely harmonious arrangement of townhouses on the Neumarkt is, surprisingly, a work of our time. Following the recent turn of the millennium, the old-city core around the Frauenkirche returned to its former beauty, mostly in the elegant baroque style. The city's important historical buildings that were destroyed by the hail of bombs that fell on Dresden in 1945 can be found once again at their original locations. With the return of these self-confident mansions, Dresden has regained much of its unmistakable character. The Heinrich-Schütz Residence and the neighboring **Köhlersche House** on the corner of Frauenstrasse are two particularly impressive reconstructions. The stately Köhlersche House with the lovely portal relief depicting work on a vineyard was built in 1745 and is one of the most superb examples of an urban rococo building.

The **Heinrich-Schütz Residence** at Neumarkt 12 was designed in 1731 by George Bähr, the same architect who built the Frauenkirche. The colorful rounded bay contains a children's frieze consisting of 32 figures, a decorative work preserved from the original Renaissance building that had belonged to the court's music director Heinrich Schütz.

Bähr also designed both the large **Hotel de Saxe** and the nearby **British Hotel** at Landhausstrasse 6, which is worth taking a look at. The stately palace from 1715 was reconstructed with preserved pieces of the original

Rococo portal frieze on the front of the Köhlersche House (Frauenstrasse 14)

Baroque townhouses on Rampische Strasse at Neumarkt

Exhibition of historic Neumarkt
Pirnaischer Platz/Landhausstrasse
daily 10am–6pm
www.neumarkt-dresden.de

▷ Tram 1, 2, 4 (Altmarkt)

The Hotel de Saxe with the monument of King Frederick Augustus II

Popular meeting place:
The Luther monument in front
of the Frauenkirche

facade. The building at Frauenkirche 16 is another embellishment of the Neumarkt.
A small shopping lane runs alongside the → **Johanneum** (Neumarkt 2) in the **Quartier an der** → **Frauenkirche**. Here, as elsewhere, modern fronts were integrated into the historical cityscape. The passageway to Rampische Strasse provides a rewarding view of the lovely baroque buildings.
The Neumarkt plaza presents monuments to King Frederick Augustus II (1867) and the reformer Martin Luther (1883), as well as the Turkish Fountain, which was created as early as 1648.

Horse-drawn carriages add a nostalgic flair to Neumarkt

Lovely Renaissance bay window
on the Heinrich Schütz Residence

The Münzgasse at the Neumarkt
entices with its many restaurants

Much-admired baroque
ensemble at the Frauenkirche

Neustadt, Äußere
Neustadt, Outer

This is Dresden's busiest, liveliest, hippest area. The **Outer Neustadt** is an El Dorado for creative and exotic personalities. The Gründerzeit buildings north of Albertplatz contain a colorful mix of cafés, bars and trendy shops. The heart of the young neighborhood is the **Kunsthofpassage** between Alaun and Görlitzer Strasse, which captivates its visitors with playful and imaginatively designed back courtyards. The courtyard "Hof der Fabelwesen" was designed by the artist Viola Schöppe in 1997. In "Hof der Elemente," water from a sky blue building wall runs every half hour through the artistically arranged rain drain. Night owls feel particularly at ease in this area of the city where the **Scheune** cultural center (Alaunstraße 36–40) is an established institution.

The **Old Jewish Cemetery** lies at Martin-Luther-Platz. Saxony's oldest existing graveyard for the Jewish community was founded in 1751 and used until 1868 (Pulsnitzer Strasse 10). It is worthwhile taking a detour to the **Kraszewski Museum**. The life and work of the Polish author Jósef Ignacy Kraszewski (1812–87) is presented in his residential home in Dresden where he lived in exile.

Kunsthofpassage
Alaunstrasse 70
www.kunsthofpassage.de

Kraszewski-Museum
Nordstrasse 28
Wed–Sun 1pm–6pm
Tel. 804 44 50
www.museen-dresden.de

▷ Tram 13 (Görlitzer Straße), 11 (Nordstraße)

19th century façades dominate the Neustadt district

A building in the Kunsthofpassage

A playful arrangement of rain drains in the Kunsthofpassage

The Outer Neustadt is a colorful, imaginative oasis

Neustadt, Innere
Neustadt, Inner

Pretty shops in pretty buildings – the (inner) Neustadt attracts visitors with its charming aristocratic flair. In 1722 Augustus the Strong had the quarter on the right side of the Elbe developed into the ideal baroque city that we see today. The original Königstrasse was designed into a boulevard leading to the → **Japanese Palace.** Pöppelmann, the architect who designed the Zwinger, also created the elegant facades. A stroll along the atmospheric passageways is enticing. The **Kunsthandwerkerpassagen** lead to Hauptstrasse, where the attractive **Kügelgen House** stands (No. 13). A **museum about the Dresden Romantic era** is situated in the former residential home of the painter Gerhard von Kügelgen (1772–1820).

A few steps away in the direction of Albertplatz stands the impressive **Dreikönigskirche,** a church built in 1739. Matthäus Daniel Pöppelmann and George Bähr, creators of the Frauenkirche, designed the baroque hall church. The tower was added in 1857. A true Dresden sculptural treasure is stored inside this house of worship: The Dance of Death, an important Renaissance frieze created around 1536 by Christoph Walter I, once adorned the palace. The church served as the Saxon state parliament building from 1990 to 1994. The famous equestrian sculpture of Augustus

Authentic baroque residential homes on Königstrasse

Museum der Dresdner Romantik
Hauptstrasse 13
Wed–Sun 10am–6pm
Tel. 804 47 60
www.museen-dresden.de

Dreikönigskirche
Hauptstrasse 23

▷ Tram 4, 8, 9 (Neustädter Markt)

Baroque glory with arcades to saunter through on Hauptstrasse

The Dreikönigskirche is a church with a moving history

Shopping in the Neustädt market hall on Ritterstrasse

the Strong stands at the Neustädter Markt. Depicted as the "**Golder Rider**," the legendary elector (1670–1733) turns towards Poland where he had also reigned as king since 1697. The monument from 1736 was designed by Jean Joseph Vinache.

In front of the Augustus Bridge stands the **Neustädter Wache**, a work designed in the strict French baroque style by Zacharias Longuelune (1739). The baroque palace at Grossen Meissner Strasse 15 is also quite marvelous.

Historic Neustädter Wache behind the Golden Rider

Von Kügelgen's painting studio in the Museum of the Romantic

Panometer
Panometer

Take a trip into Dresden's past and see what the city on the Elbe looked like during its baroque heyday. A visit to the Panometer can make this wish come true. A 360 degree monumental picture presents an overwhelming and deceivingly "real look" at a panoramic view of the Elbe city. The realistic illustration of Dresden, which is 105 meters long and 27 meters high, was created by the Berlin artist Yadegar Asisi.

Standing on a platform that represents the tower of the Catholic royal church, one looks onto the rooftops of the windy Altstadt with the palace, Frauenkirche and Zwinger: The alleyways and plazas are abounding with life on a sunny Sunday in August, 1756.

In the exhibition "1756 Dresden," originals are on display from the glorious Augustus era that came to an abrupt end when the Seven Years' War broke out (1756–63). The traditional veduta art form is revived here, too. The Asisi Panometer of Dresden is located in an industrial era monument, a former gasometer in the Reick district.

The illusion of an all-around view is perfect from the center platform

The former gasometer in Reick

Gasanstaltstrasse 8b
Tues–Fri 9am–7pm, Sat/Sun 10am–8pm
Tel. 86 03 94 0
www.asisi.de

▷ S 1, 2 (Dresden-Reick)

*View over the rooftops of
the historical center of Dresden
in 1756*

Pfunds-Molkerei
Pfunds Dairy

This is probably the best known milk store in the world. A visit to Pfunds Dairy is a high-point of almost every sightseeing tour of Dresden. Upon entering the historically furnished store, visitors are unsure what to take in first: the tasty presentation of cheese and milk products or the overwhelming colorful interior. The store counter, walls and columns are made of original majolica tiles that were custom made for the Pfund brothers' dairy by the world-famous company Villeroy & Boch in 1892.

More than 3500 tiles decorate the store including the former milk-drinking hall (a small bistro today) that resembles a majestic hall in a palace. The milk production is presented as a genre painting with putti, mythical creatures and, of course, grazing cows playing the main roles. Visitors can purchase traditional milk products as well as other specialties such as milk soap here. A cafe is located on the upper level.

Pfund Brothers' Dairy
Bautzner Strasse 79
www.pfunds.de

▷ Tram 11 (Pulsnitzer Straße)

A world to marvel: the marvelously decorated milk shop

Artistic majolica tiles and columns made by Villeroy & Boch

The dairy presents a modest exterior

Prager Strasse
Prager Strasse

Prager Strasse has been Dresden's main shopping strip since the mid-19th century. Until it was destroyed in 1945, its name was synonymous with elegant city shopping. In the mid-1960s it was rebuilt according to the preferred urban design of the time — as an overly wide pedestrian zone framed by a line of hotels and a 240-meter-long row of residential buildings. Ground-level decoration, such as the **Dandelion Fountain**, invite you to linger.

The original **Rundkino** cinema also goes back to this building period: The black and white striped rotunda by Gerhard Landgraf and Waltraud Heischkel opened in 1972. The striking decorative front, set before the façade, was forged by the graphic artist Gerhard Papstein.

Twenty-five years later, another movie theater complex opened, causing quite a stir. The **UFA-Kinozentrum** designed in a deconstructivist style by Coop Himmelb(l)au from Vienna has by now become a classic work of contemporary architecture. The foyer of this spectacular building on St. Petersburger Strasse resembles a huge, tilting crystal, which drew it international attention.

Prager Strasse returns to its original historic width on its way to the stately **Hauptbahnhof** (1898), Dresden's main train station.

Prager Strasse with the sculpture "Friendship among Nations" from 1986

▷ S 1, 2, 3 (Hauptbahnhof), Tram 8, 9, 11, 12 (Prager Strasse)

The Ufa-Kinozentrum looks like an illuminated crystal

The Rundkino with its unusual design from 1972

Raddampfer auf der Elbe
Paddle Steamers on the Elbe

The nostalgic paddle steamers are as much a part of Dresden as the Elbe itself: They anchor in front of the → **Brühlsche Terrasse** and have been operating here since the German empire. These excursion boats with paddle wheels in wheelhouses on the side are powered by steam engines, including an original machine from 1841 – the only one fueled by coal.

The oldest steamer of the fleet is the "Stadt Wehlen," christened "Dresden III" in 1879. Years ago the Sächsische Dampfschifffahrt, Saxon's boat company, did a general overhaul of its nine steamboats and had them elaborately restored. The oldest paddle steamers in the world travel between the **Übigau Palace** und the **Pillnitz Palace**. Dresden shows its best side on a city tour boat trip which passes by the → **Elbe palaces** on the hillside of Loschwitz and stops at the → **Blue Wonder** bridge.

Picturesque Elbe river viewed from the elevated level of the Elbe palaces

Station stop on the Brühlsche Terrasse in front of the Augustus Bridge

Pier
Terrassenufer 20
Tel. 86 60 90
www.saechsische-dampfschiffahrt.de

▷ Tram 4, 8, 9 (Theaterplatz), 3, 7 (Synagoge)

The oldest paddle steamers
have been on tour since 1879

The pleasure steamers run between
Pillnitz Palace and Übigau Palace

Rathausplatz
Rathaus Square

It has been a striking element of Dresden's cityscape for a century. Almost a hundred meters high, the **tower of the Rathaus**, Dresden's town hall, is a giant in a city-center devoid of high-rises. The tower is crowned by a giant, too. Hercules, the 4.9-meter-high gilded patron saint, stands on the copper roof, emptying his horn of plenty over the city. The crown on his head resembles a city wall. Both the **"Rathaus man"** and the tower are city landmarks.

The staircase hall, too, is designed in a stately and representative style. The dome is adorned by a unique Jugendstil monumental mural by the painter Otto Gussmann (1910–14).

The architects Karl Roth and Edmund Bräter designed the Rathaus in a mix of neo-baroque and Jugendstil elements. After World War II, the façades facing the Ring were reconstructed in a more simplified form.

The elegant **Gewandhaus**, built in 1768–70 in a subtle baroque style by Johann Friedrich Knöbel, borders the Rathausplatz. Originally built for a clothier, it serves today as a hotel. A lovely baroque fountain is located in back, a treasure left over from the house where the court goldsmith Johann Melchior Dinglinger once lived.

Baroque masterpiece on the front of the Gewandhaus

Rathaus Tower
Kreuzstrasse
April–Oct: 10am–6pm

Gewandhaus
Ringstrasse 1

▷ Tram 1, 2, 3, 4, 7, 12 (Pirnaischer Platz)

Lovely Jugendstil staircase hall in the foyer of the town hall tower

Old town hall tower behind the postwar entrance front

The historic Gewandhaus is a luxury hotel today

Residenzschloss
Royal Palace

The oldest museum in Germany is also one of the most valuable treasure chambers in Europe with a presentation of Ottoman art unlike any other. The Royal Palace offers a wealth of high-quality attractions.

Since 1732 the **Grüne Gewölbe** (Green Vault) has contained a breath-taking presentation of stately riches. The Historic Green Vault displays the restored collection in its original baroque design: Almost three thousand precious works of art and the most whimsical collection of precious objects in the world. In the New Green Vault visitors can admire the virtuosity of baroque jewelers' art in Dresden, including works by the court goldsmith Johann Melchior Dinglinger, who created brilliant masterpieces for Augustus the Strong. Another highlight of the palace museum is the **Turkish Chamber** with the Ottoman state tent from the 17th century and the majestic jewelry designed for kingly horses. The **Coin Cabinet** and **Kupferstichkabinett** (Collection of Prints, Drawings and Photographs) are also worth a visit.

In the near future (2011), the **Rüstkammer** (Armory) will return to the Zwinger, presenting elegant knight's armor and decorative weapons.

Schlossstrasse
Tel. 49 14 20 00
www.skd.museum
Historic Green Vault: Wed–Mon 10am–7pm
New Green Vault: until 6pm
Turkish Chamber and Kupferstichkabinett:
Wed–Mon 10am–6pm
Hausmann Tower: April–Oct: 10am–6pm
Rüstkammer (in the Painting Gallery until it moves):
Tues–Sun 10am–6pm

▷ Tram 4, 8, 9 (Theaterplatz); 1, 2, 4 (Altmarkt)

The Hausmann Tower with its baroque spire looms over the palace

The Small Palace Courtyard with the Renaissance arcade from 1588–95

*Newest attraction: the reconstructed
English Staircase*

*The Schlossplatz is dominated
by the imposing Georgentor*

The palace building is itself a work of art unifying six-hundred years of architectural history. The elector's residence is a glorious Renaissance building, demonstrated by the **sgraffiti façades** in the great palace courtyard. Caspar Voigt von Wierandt created this complex in 1548–56. The historic 101-meter-high **Hausmann Tower** has been the tallest tower in the city since 1676. The "**Schöne Pforte**," the portal of the palace chapel, is a Renaissance gem built in 1555 by Giovanni Maria from Padua.

The palace façade was redesigned into a Neo-Renaissance style by the architects Dunger and Fröhlich in 1889–1901. The **Georgentor**, the gate at the palace plaza, is especially regal with Duke Georg depicted on horseback in the gable. A modern accent was added in 2009 when a transparent dome was built over **the small palace courtyard**.

"Moor with Emerald Plate"
(1724) by Balthasar Permoser

Treasures of the elector in the
Jewel Room of the Green Vault

Ottoman state tent and horse jewelry
in the Turkish Chamber

The royal household of the Grand Mogul
Aureng Zeb by Dinglinger (1701–08)

Silver-gilt room in the Green Vault

Sächsischer Landtag
Saxon State Parliament

Another one of Dresden's attractions is the building ensemble on the Elbe consisting of the Saxon parliament building and Congress Center. When these modern structures were constructed, the famous Altstadt riverbank promenade was extended downstream. The Saxon Landtag, erected in 1991–94 behind the Semper opera house, was the first new parliament building to be created for a federal state in the east after German reunification in 1990. The architect Peter Kulka created a transparent building. For the plenary hall he adopted a variation of a motif from the world-famous architect Mies van der Rohe. The **International Congress Center Dresden** (ICCD) that opened in 2004 is connected to it. What makes this building so unusual and interesting is the slightly rising terrace along the Elbe which, like the Brühlsche Terrasse, leads to a broad outdoor staircase. The design was a work by the architects Storch, Ehlers and Partner.

The hundred-year-old **Erlwein-Speicher**, named after its architect Hans Erlwein, rises up between the two new buildings. It was once one of the most modern storage build-ings in the city. Today this historical monu-ment operates as a luxury hotel for the convention center.

Entrance to the Saxon parliament building that opened in 1994

Curvaceous International Congress Center

Bernhard-von-Lindenau-Platz

Hotel and Congress Center
Devrientstrasse 10–12
www.dresden-congresscenter.de

▷ Tram 6, 11 (Kongresszentrum)

The Finance Office of 1928–31 is part of the parliament building

Schloss Pillnitz
Pillnitz Palace

Pillnitz is the most fascinating palace complex in all of Dresden. The summer residence of the Saxon rulers continues to captivate us today with its exotic charm. What looks like the work of a single hand was actually developed over a period of many centuries. Matthäus Daniel Pöppelmann set the standard in 1720/21 when he built the fanciful **Water Palace** right on the Elbe in the Chinese fashion of the times. Most of the picturesque rooftop chimneys are mere decoration. Chinese motifs also adorn the orange façade and an outdoor staircase leads to the Gondola Harbor. Its companion piece, the **Mountain Palace,** was erected in 1723/24.

Pillnitz is a fairytale palace of the Saxon court; here the Mountain Palace

Augustus the Strong's baroque-chinois pleasure palaces were enlarged in 1788–91. When Christian Friedrich Schuricht built the **New Palace** in 1818–26, the palace complex with its three wings was complete. The **Palace Museum** is located within the tasteful classical halls. The **Arts and Crafts Museum** is inside the Mountain and Water Palaces. The expansive **Palace Park** grounds contain more than two thousand trees and shrubs, six hundred potted plants and a Palm Tree House (1861). The Camellia tree from Japan, more than two hundred years old, is a real star, displaying up to 35,000 crimson blossoms from mid-February to mid-April.

Classicist design of the Catholic court chapel in the New Palace

August-Böckstiegel-Str. 2
Tel. 261 32 60
www.schloesser-dresden.de

Park: from 5am until dusk
Palace Museum: April–Oct: Tues–Sun 10am–5pm
Arts and Crafts Museum: May–Oct: 10am–6pm
(Mnt. Palace: closed Mon; Water Palace: closed Tues)

▷ Tram 6, 12 (Schillerplatz), then Bus 83

The New Palace with clock tower connecting the Water and Mountain Palaces

The elector's ship docked on the Elbe at the Water Palace

Semperoper
Semper Opera

The Semper Opera is a world-famous land-mark of Dresden and one of the most beauti-ful theater houses in all of Europe. The building master Gottfried Semper (1803–79) had already won over the hearts of the Dres-deners when he built the first court theater between the → **Zwinger** and the Elbe. When the structure from 1841 burned down, he was summoned again. Semper, a revolutionary in the Dresden May Uprising of 1849, had been forced to flee and live abroad.

This grand monumental structure was created from 1871–78 in the Italian High Renaissance style. In addition to its superb acoustics, the opera house is praised for its decorative am-bulatories and staircases, furnished with stucco marble, precious metals and murals. The majestic portal is crowned by the bronze panther quadriga created by Johannes Schilling. The sculptures of the poet laureates Goethe and Schiller at the entrance originally stood in the first court theater (Ernst Rietschel). Destroyed again in World War II, the splendid structure was rebuilt true to the original and with a careful eye for detail under the direc-tion of Wolfgang Hänsch in 1977–85. Only the audience hall was modified slightly. Composers such as Carl Maria von Weber, Richard Wagner and Richard Strauss wrote opera history in Dresden.

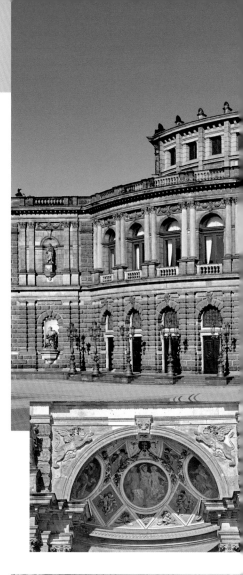

Saxon State Opera House of Dresden
Theaterplatz 2
www.semperoper.de
Mon–Thurs 10am–6pm, Friday until 7pm;
Sat/Sun 10am–5pm

▷ Tram 4, 8, 9 (Theaterplatz)

The Saxon state opera house, named after its builder

Magnificent opera hall with the king's box

The calotte above the portal depicting the three graces

Glorious staircase hall with stucco marble columns

Striezelmarkt
Striezel Christmas Market

During the Christmas season, this Dresden attraction draws millions of visitors to the → **Altmarkt** each year. In existence since at least 1434, the Stiezelmarkt is the oldest Christmas market in Germany. The unique market got its name from the most famous Dresdener of all – the popular German fruit cake known as "Stollen" or "Striezel." The pope gave his blessing in 1492 for the most important ingredient, butter.

Even Augustus the Strong took a fancy to this tasty cake. In 1730 this royal Striezel enthusiast had a huge fruit cake, weighing over a ton, baked especially for an army camp. The gesture is commemorated each year by the Stollenfest, when the local bakers' guild bakes the longest Christmas Stollen in the world.

A world record became the symbol of the Striezelmarkt: the traditional step pyramid from the Erz Mountains is 14 meters high and decorated with 42 wooden figures.

This festive spectacle with 250 stands offering an array of treats in addition to the Stollen, such as Pulsnitz gingerbread and dried fruit dolls, comes to a close on December 24.

A little warmth during the cold Christmas season

Altmarkt 2
Late November to Dec 24
Sun–Thurs 10am–8pm, Fri/Sat 10am–9pm
www.striezel-markt.de

▷ Tram 1, 2, 4 (Altmarkt)

Fairytale setting of booths and carousel

Bright decorative lights before Christmas at the Altmarkt

Sweets and cookies made by hand

Taschenberg-Palais
Taschenberg Palace

The Taschenberg Palace, a magnificent baroque structure, has been the most posh hostel in Dresden for three hundred years, providing a domicile to numerous Saxon heirs and regents. Augustus the Strong originally had the estate built right next to his palace in 1705–08 for his mistress Anna Constanze von Hoym, better known as the Countess Cosel. At that time the luxurious love nest, designed by Johann Friedrich Karcher, consisted merely of the center structure with the richly decorated façade and balconies.

Between 1756 and 1767 Julius Heinrich Schwarze and Christian Friedrich Exner added two side wings with stylish courts of honor, making it the most magnificent palace in the city and its rococo furnishings a legend. Following an elaborate reconstruction in 1995, the elegance and luxury of the Taschenberg Palace has returned as an exclusive hotel. The historic rooms of the Blue Cabinet and the impressive baroque staircase were also reconstructed at that time.

Gottfried Semper's Neo-Gothic **Cholera Fountain** was erected in 1843 on the plaza between the hotel and the Zwinger.

The neo-baroque **Schauspielhaus** (1911–13) with its magnificient audience hall stands on Postplatz.

This magnificent royal entrance now leads into a luxury hotel

Rococo façade of the Taschenberg Palace

Hotel Taschenbergpalais
Taschenberg 3

▷ Tram 1, 2, 4, 8, 9, 11, 12 (Postplatz)

*The Schauspielhaus not far
from the palace*

*The reconstructed Schauspielhaus
audience hall*

Technische Sammlungen
Technical Collections

When technology is presented in an interesting and lively way, it is fun and becomes an enthralling experience for visitors. The forerunners of the media age fascinate both young and old at the site where the best cameras in the world were once produced. In the Technical Collections, visitors can admire an array of objects ranging from replicas of the first adding machines created by Wilhelm Schickardt and Gottfried Wilhelm Leibniz in the 17th century to epoch-making computer old-timers – and also the whole breadth of historic photo and cinema technology. This diverse museum is located in the former camera factory of the Ernemann Company which was founded in 1897. It became the Zeiss Ikon Company in 1927. Beginning in 1959 four decades of classic Pentacon cameras were manufactured here. The collection makes clear how important Dresden was in the precision and electro-technical industries. The wonderful world of animated cartoons from the DEFA-Studios is also on display. Scientific and technical phenomena are explained to young visitors in the Mathematics Discovery World and in the Experimental Field.
There is a lovely view of the city from the café in the 48-meter-high **Ernemann Tower**.

Museum building with the compact Ernemann Tower

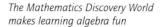

The Mathematics Discovery World makes learning algebra fun

Junghansstrasse 1–3
Tues–Fri 9am–5pm, Sat/Sun 10am–6pm
Tel. 488 72 72
www.tsd.de

▷ Tram 4, 10, Bus 61 (Pohlandplatz)

An exhibition object from the early days of the computer

A movie projector made in Dresden

Leading technology: a camera made in Saxony

Theaterplatz
Theaterplatz

Grand buildings demand a spacious arena. Several structures of high distinction are presented around Theaterplatz including the → **Painting Gallery**, the → **Semper Opera**, the → **Catholic Royal Court Church** and the → **Royal Palace**, making it one of the loveliest squares in all of Europe. The small temple structure at its center hardly even gets noticed, but the **Altstädter Wache** is the creative work of a luminary architect: Karl Friedrich Schinkel, Prussia's famous architect, designed this little treasure in 1830–32 in the classicist style. The main theater ticket office is located behind the sandstone columns.

On the side of the square facing the Elbe stands the **Italienische Dörfchen**, the Italian village, which is really just a building for gastronomy. The curious name recalls the builders and artisans from Italy who took up their living quarters here in the 18th century when they were building the baroque court church. The guesthouse on the Elbe, designed in 1913 by the city's building councilor Hans Erlwein, applied all the styles that were already present on Theaterplatz.

The **equestrian sculpture** in the center of the square depicts King Johann, who sat on the throne of Saxony in 1854–73. It was created by the sculptor Johannes Schilling in 1883.

The Altstädter Wache is a classicist structure

Altstädter Wache
Theaterplatz

Italienisches Dörfchen
Theaterplatz 3

▷ Tram 4, 8, 9 (Theaterplatz)

Restaurant looking onto the Elbe:
The "Italian Village"

King Johann looks upon the Royal
Church and Royal Palace

Trinitatisfriedhof
Trinity Cemetery

They designed gravestones for this cemetery and later found their own resting place here: Caspar David Friedrich, the great Romantic painter, and Ernst Rietschel, an important sculptor. Many important figures from Dresden are buried at the Trinitatisfriedhof, a cemetery that was established in 1815 in what is today the Johannstadt district. They include Carl Gustav Carus (painter and philosopher), Friedrich Kind (lyricist for the Freischütz Opera), Otto Ludwig (novel writer), Julius Otto (conductor of the Kreuz choir), Wilhelmine Schröder-Devrient (opera singer), Friedrich Wieck (musician and father of Clara Schumann) and Georg Wrba (sculptor). The architect Constantin Lipsius and Dr. Friedrich Struve, the inventor of artificial mineral water, are also buried here.

The obelisk next to the main entrance was erected in honor of the fallen revolutionaries of the May Uprising of 1849.

The classicist entrance gate was made by Gottlieb Friedrich Thormeyer and eternalized by Caspar David Friedrich in his painting "Cemetery Entrance."

Final resting place of famous people from Dresden

The grave of the painter Caspar David Friedrich (1774–1840)

Corner of Fiedler and Gerokstrasse
daily 8am–8pm, closes at 4pm in winter

▷ Tram 6 (Trinitatisplatz)

Gravesite of the architect
Constantin Lipsius (1832–94)

A place for outdoor prayer services

Weinberge in Radebeul
Vineyards in Radebeul

Dresden is a city that pleases all the senses, including the taste buds. The local wines are a treat to the palate. The Saxon Weinstrasse runs through Dresden to the neighboring **Radebeul**, where grapes have been cultivated for over six hundred years. The vineyard of **Schloss Wackerbarth**, the castle that Graf von Wackerbarth built for his retirement in 1727–31, lies in a romantic setting. The Saxon state wine-growing estate offers tours and wine-tasting, sells its products and runs a guest house.

The **Weinbaumuseum Hoflößnitz,** a museum located in the wine-making estate of the elector of 1650, is dedicated to the history of wine-growing in one of Europe's most northern vineyards. The estate is also a special example of Dresden architecture. The baroque lifestyle of the Saxon sovereigns that was lost in Dresden has been preserved here in the original. The eighty Brazilian birds adorning the ceiling are unusual and precious, painted by the court painter Albert van Eyckhout. A stairway leads to the top of the vineyard where a restaurant in the **Spitzhaus** is located in the distance.

Precious baroque painting on the elector's estate in Hoflößnitz

Schloss Wackerbarth
Wackerbarthstr. 1
daily 9:30am–8pm
www.schloss-wackerbarth.de

▷ S 1 (Radebeul-West), Tram 4 (Schloss Wackerbarth)

Weinbaumuseum Hoflößnitz
Knohllweg 37
Tues–Sun April–Oct: 10am–5pm, Nov–March: 12pm–4pm
www.hofloessnitz.de

▷ S 1 (Radebeul-Weintraube), Tram 4 (Wasastrasse)

The Belvedere of Wackerbarth
Castle in front of the Radebeul
vineyard

Hoflößnitz wine-growing museum
in an attractive setting

Wackerbarth Castle guarantees
fine Saxon wine

Yenidze
Yenidze

Yenidze is probably Dresden's most bizarre landmark and one of the most unusual structures in all of Germany. The once highly efficient cigarette factory looks like an oriental mosque today.

A century ago, the tobacco mogul Hugo Zietz wanted to create a memorable corporate identity. For his "Yenidze Oriental Tobacco and Cigarette Factory," named for the Ottoman area where the tobacco was grown, he erected a magnificent building right out of Arabian Nights in 1907–12. The tobacco mosque on the Elbe was modeled after the monumental gravesite of a caliph in Cairo. The architect Hermann Martin Hammitzsch designed seven exotic-looking ventilation shafts, a chimney that resembles a minaret and a Moorish-style façade. The centerpiece of the factory building is the dazzling glass dome (18 meters high) where Dresden's highest restaurant is located and cabaret is performed.

Dresdener's are now quite proud of the building, but it was very controversial when it was built. Production stopped in 1952. Today the tourist attraction behind the railway embankment near the Marien Bridge is an office building.

A storyteller in the colorful
Yenidze dome

Weißeritzstrasse 3
Restaurant in the dome open daily at 11 am.
Tel. 490 59 90
www.kuppelrestaurant.de

▷ S 1, 2 (Dresden-Mitte), Tram 6, 11 (Kongresszentrum)

Illuminated landmark of
oriental architecture

Oriental dancing instead of tobacco
in the old tobacco mosque

The former cigarette factory
is close to the Altstadt

Zwinger
Zwinger

We owe Dresden's contribution to world heritage to the brilliance of the architect Matthäus Daniel Pöppelmann and the sculptor Balthasar Permoser, who created this unique rococo masterpiece from 1709 to 1728. Dresden's most famous architectural structure began as an orangery for a palace that was never realized. Numerous citrus trees used to adorn the courtyards of the Zwinger, whose name refers to its position between two fortification walls.

Augustus the Strong had the winter quarters of his favorite trees developed into an imposing fairground for his son's wedding in 1710. The majestic **Crown Gate** at the Zwinger moat, symbolizes his regality in Poland.

The **Wall Pavilion** provides a climax to the grounds' aesthetics: Abundant with figures, it stresses the side of the Zwinger facing away from the city where the **Nymph's Bath**, a place of sensual merriment, lies hidden.

Its mirror image, the **City Pavilion**, stands across from the Wall Pavilion with chimes made of Meissen porcelain. Here is the entrance to the magnificent **Porcelain Collection**. After the era of lavish celebrations came to a close, the Zwinger became a museum complex of which the **Mathematics and Physics Room** is also a part. When Semper built the → **Painting Gallery**, the Zwinger was complete.

Sophienstrasse
Tel. 491 420 00
www.sdk.museum

Porcelain Collection
Tues–Sun 10am–6pm
Mathematics and Physics Room Re-opening 2011

▷ Tram 4, 8, 9 (Theaterplatz) and 1, 2, 11, 12 (Postplatz)

*Fountains and sculptures
in the Nymph's Bath*

*The Glockenspiel Pavilion on
the city-side of the Zwinger*

*The Wall Pavilion is an
unsurpassed rococo masterpiece*

*Porcelain collection with precious
pieces from East Asia and Meissen*

*Zwinger ceremonial court with
the Painting Gallery*

Index of Highlights

Index of People

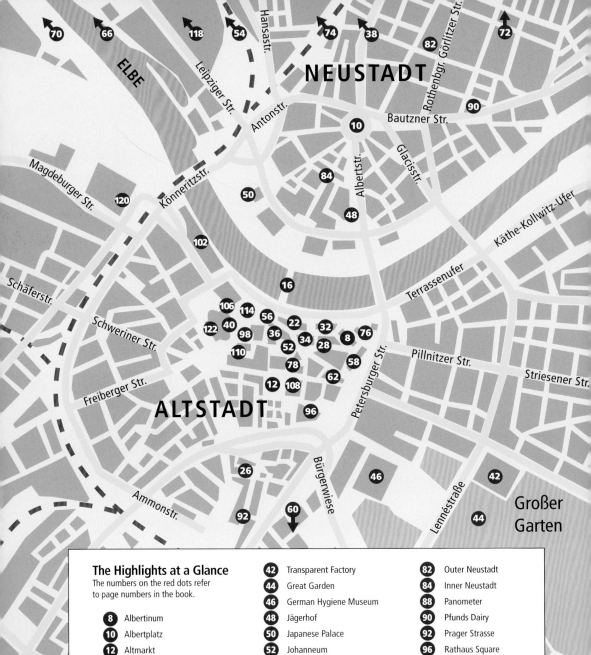

The Highlights at a Glance

The numbers on the red dots refer to page numbers in the book.